The Wood Design Awards 2004

A NORTH AMERICAN PROGRAM OF ARCHITECTURAL EXCELLENCE

Tuns Press
Faculty of Architecture and Planning
Dalhousie University
P.O. Box 1000
Halifax, Nova Scotia
Canada B3J 2X4
tunspress.dal.ca

The Wood Design Awards 2004

Editor: Don Griffith, Janam Publications Inc.
Design: M. N. Manseau / M. N. Massé, Janam Publications Inc.
Production: Donald Westin
Printing: Friesens

© 2004 Tuns Press and Janam Publications Inc.
All Rights Reserved. Published January 2005
Printed in Canada

National Library of Canada Cataloguing in Publication

Wood Design Awards 2004 / edited by Don Griffith.

ISSN 1708-5233 The Wood Design Awards
ISBN 0-929112-52-0

1. Building, Wooden–Canada.
2. Building, Wooden–United States.
3. Architecture–Awards–Canada.
4. Architecture–Awards–United States.
5. Architecture–Canada–21st century.
6. Architecture–United States–21st century.
I. Griffith, Don

NA4110.W66 2004   721'.0448'097109051   C2003-905316-4

Cover: Big Ten Burrito Restaurant, Ply Architecture   Photo. Howard Doughty

The Wood Design Awards is the only North American-wide Program to recognize and award excellence in wood architecture. The annual Program is open to new and remodeled residential and non-residential projects and building interiors from the U.S. and Canada. Awarded projects challenge conventional thinking about the construction and architectural uses of wood. This book, one of a series published annually, is a lasting reference of fresh ideas.

The 12 projects selected from 189 submissions of the 2004 Wood Design Awards cover the most diverse range of work since the Program's inauguration in 2001. For the first time, three interior projects, an historic building restoration, and a factory modular home were among those chosen by the jury. All 12 projects embody a high level of construction in the most common building scales, and stand as examples of some the best architectural design in the U.S. and Canada.

The Wood Design Awards is offered by Wood Design & Building and Wood Le Bois magazines [www.woodmags.com], and managed by Janam Publications Inc. We gratefully acknowledge the support of our sponsors and supporting associations: Structurlam Products Inc., Open Joist 2000, Minwax, The Hardwood Council, the Western Red Cedar Lumber Association, the Canadian Wood Council, and the Canadian Plywood Association.

Don Griffith
Coordinator, *The Wood Design Awards*

The Wood Design Awards

2004 Sponsors

www.structurlam.com

www.minwax.com

www.openjoist2000.com

Supporting Associations

www.cwc.ca

www.canply.org

www.realcedar.org

www.hardwoodcouncil.com

Vincent James, AIA, Principal
VJAA Inc.,
Minneapolis, Minnesota

Patricia Patkau, FRAIC,
[Hon.] FAIA, Partner
Patkau Architects Inc.,
Vancouver, British Columbia

Mark Simon, FAIA, Partner
Centerbrook Architects and Planners,
Centerbrook, Connecticut

[Photo: Roy Grogan]

The 2004 Jury

Vincent James began his firm in 1990, and since then VJAA has been recognized for its innovative, high-quality buildings. The firm's work has been published in books, monographs and periodicals, and has received nine national design awards within the past seven years. In 2001 he received the American Academy of Arts and Letters Award for Architecture, and is an Adjunct Professor at Harvard University's Graduate School of Design.

Patricia Patkau founded Patkau Architects Inc. with husband John in 1978. The firm has risen to prominence, winning numerous design awards. As lead designer, Patkau meets directly with clients to create designs that meet their aspirations and budgets. She is also a professor at the University of British Columbia, and has lectured at over 30 institutions and events throughout the world.

Mark Simon is a partner in Centerbrook Architects and Planners LLC, a firm of 65 established in 1975. It received the AIA Firm Award for 1998 based on an established reputation for architecture that has a fresh, uplifting appeal, whether vernacular or modern in style. He has taught at Yale, Harvard, the University of Maryland, Carnegie Mellon, and North Carolina University, and served as Chair of the AIA Honors Award Program.

Table of Contents

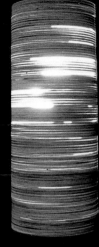

Big Ten Burrito Restaurant

PLY ARCHITECTURE

The interior of the Big Ten Burrito Restaurant emerged from questions about the relationship between the craft of making things and new technologies of digital fabrication, specifically the computer numerically-controlled [CNC] cutting and routering of standard 4x8 plywood concrete forming sheets to create complexity while minimizing construction costs and conserving the integrity of the panels.

The ceiling, walls, and floor make monolithic use of red that gives a distinct presence from the street and a strong contrasting background for the grooved patterns and other objects. The surface patterns cut into the plywood define two zones within the dining area – a space for the table and a space for the takeout counter. The takeout counter, table, and lights are the key objects.

Panels were screwed directly to the walls to conserve floor space, and to strapping on the ceiling. While the locations of the panel joints necessarily relate to the dimensions of the room, the CNC routered pattern is not confined to the limits of a 4x8 panel, but intentionally runs across the panel joints to define spatially the zones for the dining table and takeout counter. The surface pattern in the ceiling and wall panels is a complex series of grooves that vary in both plan and section where the width increases with the depth of cut. The pattern is further defined with frequency of the lines – the lines move closer together to make the hole for the lights, and farther apart and cut through the plywood at the side window and to make the hvac diffusers.

The takeout / cash register counter stands as a distinct object within the red field and defines the back edge of the dining space. Here, a series of identically sized 18mm-thick plywood tiles were CNC milled to create a shallow, relief topography of grooves and high spots that, like the walls and ceiling, flow across and suppress the joints, giving privilege to the surface.

Jury – This small project explores the possibilities of what wood can do. It is a marriage of common materials and digital machining technology that leads to creative results within a confined space.

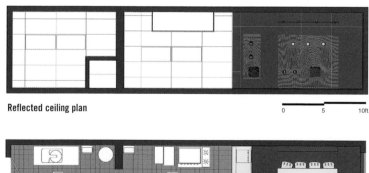

Reflected ceiling plan

0   5   10ft.

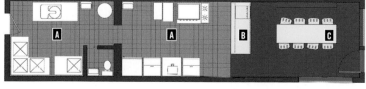

Plan   A   Kitchen   B   Take-out counter   C   Eat-in area

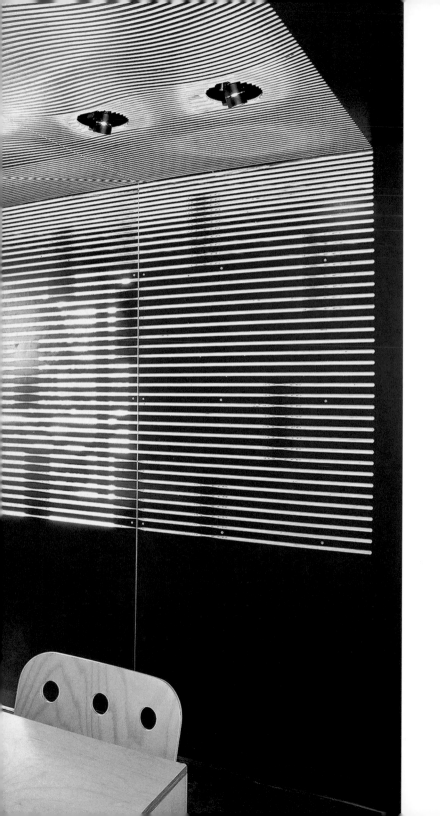

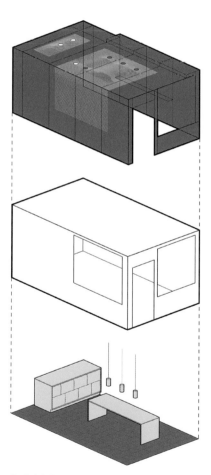

Exploded view

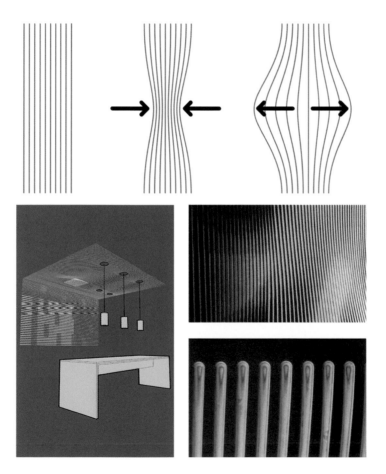

Interior
– Custom fabricated ceiling and wall panels of CNC [computer numerically-controlled] surface routered Finnform concrete forming plywood, with red color arising from phenolic resin coated surface; service counter CNC surface routed birch veneer plywood finished with polyurethane; custom fabricated pendant lights laminated birch veneer plywood rings finished with polyurethane.

Cutting patterns
A round bit was found to be the best for cutting the desired grooved pattern into the surface of the plywood because the grooves would widen as the depth of cut increased. The grooves move closer together to make the hole for the lights, and farther apart and cut through the plywood at the side window and to make the hvac diffuser. The grooves intentionally disregard the limitations of the sheet size by flowing across the panel joints. The overall pattern incorporates the lighting and hvac into a continuous field of lines, unifying the details within the small space.

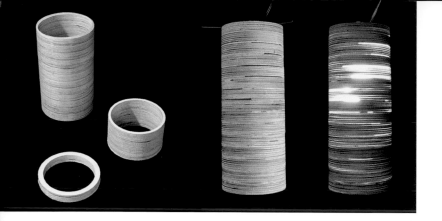

The lamp shades consist of CNC-routered plywood rings glued together. The thickness decreases at the location of the bulb so that light diffuses through the shade.

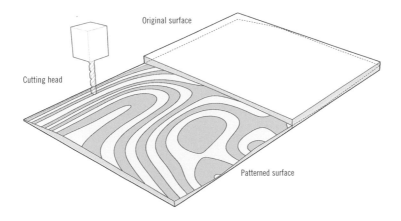

Cutting head

Original surface

Patterned surface

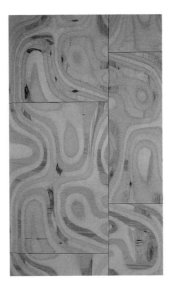

Routered pattern, front of takeout counter

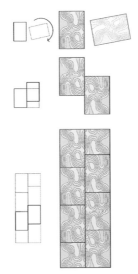

Panels oriented so that the CNC-machined patterns flow across the joints

CLIENT
Big Ten Burrito Restaurant
Ann Arbor, Michigan

ARCHITECT
Ply Architecture
[Karl Daubmann and Craig Borum
Principals; Carl Lorenz, Pete Stavenger,
Maria Walker]
Ann Arbor, Michigan

GENERAL CONTRACTOR
Ply Architecture
Ann Arbor, Michigan

PHOTOS
Howard Doughty
Bay Village, Ohio

Cognito Films

RANDALL STOUT ARCHITECTS, INC.

Cognito Films, a production company specializing in TV commercials for national brands, needed an office that demonstrated the creativity of its business, while providing the functionality for fast-paced work.

Located in Culver City, near Los Angeles, the project is an interior re-use of an 11,312sf warehouse, with an unusually high timber bowstring truss system. The interior consists of a reception area, offices, conference rooms, employee café/lounge, production pits, film editing bays, media room and tape library.

The central boardroom, workrooms and overhead staff lounge anchor the new interior. Arranged as though under continual construction, an expressive assembly of stacked 12x12 timbers physically defines the boardroom, workrooms and lounge, while suggesting the dynamic interchange between the staff and clients. The timbers do not completely enclose these areas, allowing a visual connection with the rest of the interior. An elevated staff lounge permits users to experience an impressive view of the original bowstring trusses.

The visual weight and randomness of the timbers invite the individual to pause and investigate the seemingly familiar stacked wood composition, that nevertheless delivers a fresh perspective and energy of unresolved form and space. A mezzanine provides a backdrop of staff offices and frees the plan to allow the timbers to stand as a sculptural object.

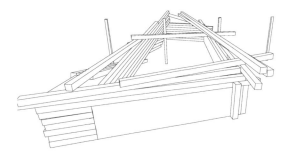

The heavy timbers used for the project came from a local lumberyard and were selected from their in-stock supply of "boxed heart" Douglas fir. Timber lengths range typically from 14ft. to 33ft., with the latter length used in the inclined stack wall that borders the ramp to the overhead staff lounge. The connections include combinations of steel angles, saddles and splice plates with 3/4-in. dia. bolts. Stacked timbers were drilled through on 7ft. centers to receive 3 in. dia. steel pipe and also glued along their entire lengths to satisfy lateral load and seismic requirements. No finish was applied, leaving the wood grain fully open to sight and touch.

Jury – A seemingly primitive building technology, as in the building of a fort, but sophisticated in its creation of artful simplicity and space that celebrates the tectonic quality of timber. The arrangement and connections are so simple that one can imagine the stacked timbers re-used at some time in the future.

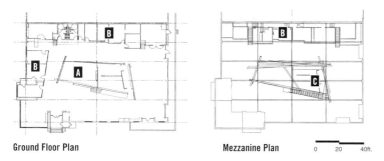

Ground Floor Plan   **Mezzanine Plan**   0   20   40ft.

A   Boardroom/ work rooms
B   Offices
C   Staff lounge

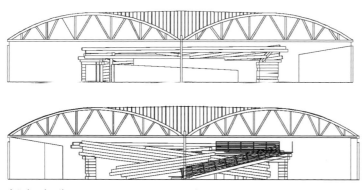

Interior elevations

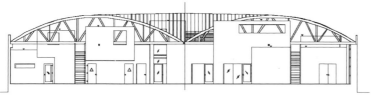

Mezzanine Elevation

Product Specs

Frame
– Existing: Poured concrete walls, timber bowstring trusses with wood roof joists

New: Douglas fir timber, 12x12 by 14ft. to 33ft. long threaded by steel pipe columns, 3in. dia. and glued along their lengths

Interior
– Sealed concrete slab on grade; partition walls of metal stud and gypsum board or plywood, steel tube frame with polycarbonate translucent panels

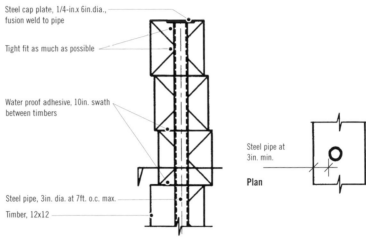

Steel cap plate, 1/4-in.x 6in.dia., fusion weld to pipe

Tight fit as much as possible

Water proof adhesive, 10in. swath between timbers

Steel pipe, 3in. dia. at 7ft. o.c. max.

Timber, 12x12

Steel pipe at 3in. min.

Plan

Section and plan assembly of stacked timber wall

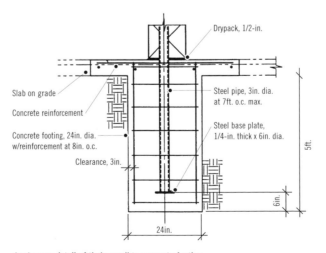

Drypack, 1/2-in.

Slab on grade

Concrete reinforcement

Concrete footing, 24in. dia. w/reinforcement at 8in. o.c.

Clearance, 3in.

Steel pipe, 3in. dia. at 7ft. o.c. max.

Steel base plate, 1/4-in. thick x 6in. dia.

5ft.

6in.

24in.

Anchorage detail of timber wall to concrete footing

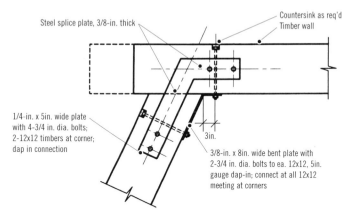

Steel splice plate, 3/8-in. thick

Countersink as req'd
Timber wall

1/4-in. x 5in. wide plate
with 4-3/4 in. dia. bolts;
2-12x12 timbers at corner;
dap in connection

3in.

3/8-in. x 8in. wide bent plate with
2-3/4 in. dia. bolts to ea. 12x12, 5in.
gauge dap-in; connect at all 12x12
meeting at corners

Plan view of connections at intersection of stacked walls

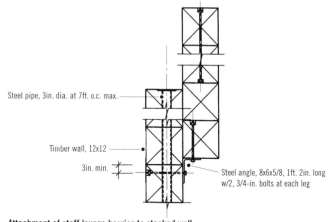

Steel pipe, 3in. dia. at 7ft. o.c. max.

Timber wall, 12x12

3in. min.

Steel angle, 8x6x5/8, 1ft. 2in. long
w/2, 3/4-in. bolts at each leg

Attachment of staff lounge barrier to stacked wall

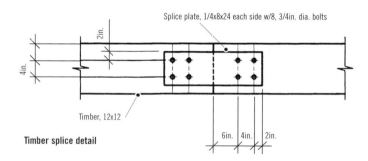

Splice plate, 1/4x8x24 each side w/8, 3/4in. dia. bolts

2in.

4in.

Timber, 12x12

6in. 4in. 2in.

Timber splice detail

CLIENT
Cognito Films
Culver City, California

ARCHITECT
Randall Stout Architects, Inc.
Los Angeles, California

STRUCTURAL ENGINEER
John A. Martin & Associates
Los Angeles, California

GENERAL CONTRACTOR
Crommie Construction Corporation
Los Angeles, California

PHOTOS
Joshua White
Culver City, California

Long Residence

CUTLER ANDERSON ARCHITECTS

Set on a wooded site on the north shore of Orcas Island, Washington, the 2,035sf residence accommodates a couple and their occasional guests. A simple shed roof opens the residence completely to the water and main part of the site, then slopes back to close it off from the easement road above.

The structure of the building is fully displayed. While not unusual to see log construction used on wooded sites, the logs are expressed in a fresh, non-traditional way. The log assemblies, consisting of log roof beams and log tripod columns, were pre-built off site in the builder's shop, then shipped and erected on site with minimal disturbance. The tripod columns fit into the log beams using concealed steel plates and bolts, and provide the required lateral stability without further need of beam-to-column bracing.

Doubled 2x8 rafters span from the rear wall to the central log beam from where 2x12 rafters take over to span the greater distance to the front window wall. The rafters rest on 4x4 plates scribed and mechanically fixed into the tops of the log beams at varying depths depending on the diameters of the logs at any given location. The short legs of tripod columns at the rear wall attach to exposed steel plates. The full-height columns punch through the floor, made obvious by a scribe line and shadow that produce a reveal around the column at the floor. The column extends down to a steel connection at the footing. The roof is built-up decking over the rafters, 2x6 framing and rigid insulation, 1/2-in. plywood and a metal roof.

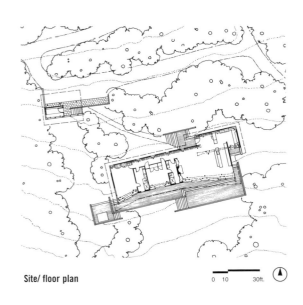

Site/ floor plan

0   10   30ft.

The whole of the wooden support system is enclosed in a glass and cedar shingle shell that protects it, and in so doing, honors it. The cedar tripods are placed directly in front of the uphill facing windows so that guests can get a sense of the building's structure as they descend to the entry. Interior millwork is Douglas fir and hardwood floors are beech.

Jury – An elegant house in which the clear heirarchy of the primary and secondary wood framing, and the transparency of the glazing prevents the structure from overpowering. The innovation of the tripod columns offers the nostalgia of a lean-to while providing a modern, simple connection to the roof, making it appear to float.

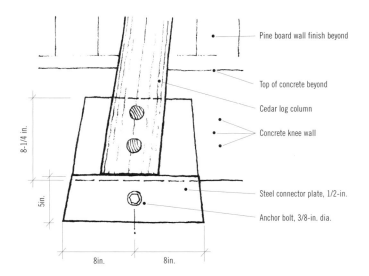

Pine board wall finish beyond

Top of concrete beyond

Cedar log column

Concrete knee wall

Steel connector plate, 1/2-in.

Anchor bolt, 3/8-in. dia.

8-1/4 in.

5in.

8in.   8in.

Elevation, column base connection

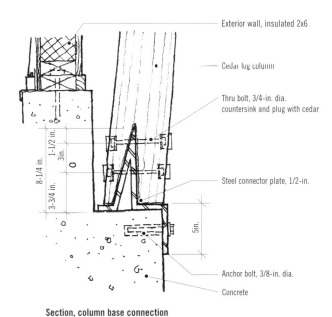

Exterior wall, insulated 2x6

Cedar log column

Thru bolt, 3/4-in. dia.
countersink and plug with cedar

Steel connector plate, 1/2-in.

Anchor bolt, 3/8-in. dia.

Concrete

8-1/4 in.

1-1/2 in.

3in.

3-3/4 in.

5in.

Section, column base connection

Product Specs

Frame
– Exposed Douglas fir rafters 2x12 and 2x8, western red cedar logs as roof beams supported on log tripod columns, roof construction: western red cedar tongue and groove 1x deck with 2x6 framing, rigid insulation and 1/2-in. plywood, finished with metal roof; tripod to log beam connection concealed steel plate, 1/2-in. dia. thru bolts countersunk and plugged with cedar, tripod base connection with steel plate, 3/8-in. and anchor bolt, 3/8-in. dia.

Exterior
– Shingle siding, western red cedar Blue Label, windows anodized aluminum attached to Douglas fir framing, custom built by contractor

Interior
– Walls pine, white washed stained, ceiling Douglas fir 1x6, floor beech, urethane finish, board-formed concrete; Douglas fir cabinetry and millwork

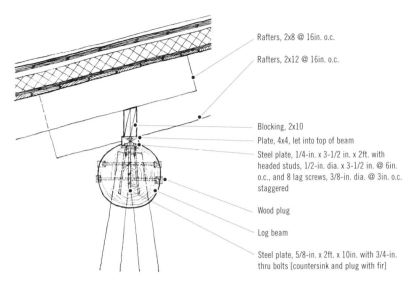

Rafters, 2x8 @ 16in. o.c.

Rafters, 2x12 @ 16in. o.c.

Blocking, 2x10

Plate, 4x4, let into top of beam

Steel plate, 1/4-in. x 3-1/2 in. x 2ft. with headed studs, 1/2-in. dia. x 3-1/2 in. @ 6in. o.c., and 8 lag screws, 3/8-in. dia. @ 3in. o.c. staggered

Wood plug

Log beam

Steel plate, 5/8-in. x 2ft. x 10in. with 3/4-in. thru bolts [countersink and plug with fir]

Section through log beam to tripod connection

ARCHITECT
Cutler Anderson Architects [Jim Cutler FAIA, Julie Montgomery AIA, Chad Harding]
Bainbridge Island, Washington

STRUCTURAL ENGINEER
Coffman Engineers
Spokane, Washington

GENERAL CONTRACTOR
Alford Homes
Poulsbo, Washington

PHOTOS
Art Grice Photography
Bainbridge Island, Washington

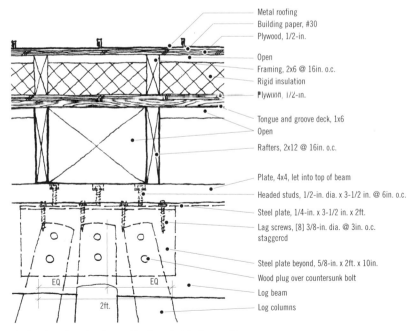

Metal roofing

Building paper, #30

Plywood, 1/2-in.

Open

Framing, 2x6 @ 16in. o.c.

Rigid insulation

Plywood, 1/2-in.

Tongue and groove deck, 1x6

Open

Rafters, 2x12 @ 16in. o.c.

Plate, 4x4, let into top of beam

Headed studs, 1/2-in. dia. x 3-1/2 in. @ 6in. o.c.

Steel plate, 1/4-in. x 3-1/2 in. x 2ft.

Lag screws, [8] 3/8-in. dia. @ 3in. o.c. staggered

Steel plate beyond, 5/8-in. x 2ft. x 10in.

Wood plug over countersunk bolt

Log beam

Log columns

EQ   EQ

2ft.

Section through roof, rafter, and log beam to tripod connection

Abbe Science Center, Solebury School

HILLIER ARCHITECTURE

The 75-year old private preparatory school occupies 99 acres in Solebury Township of Bucks County, Pennsylvania, serving 200 boarding and day students in grades 7 to 12. Built around the original farmhouse and established trees, its buildings have the scale and character of a rural village, and a strong connection with the surrounding nature.

The new 13,500sf Abbe Science Center maintains these qualities with a single-story L-shaped plan that forms a three-sided courtyard with the library. It exploits the north-south, east-west axes to maximize daylighting and passive solar gain. Lined with oversized glass doors, the single-loaded corridors give direct and literal connections to the outside.

The steel frame Science Center houses four science classrooms, four general classrooms, a greenhouse, teacher work areas and support facilities. Infrastructure includes wired and wireless networks, and individually zoned HVAC systems. A two-story student lounge, located at the confluence of the two wings, serves as the hub for informal meetings between students and instructors.

Real Cedar

The Real Cedar Design Excellence Award, given for the first time by the Western Red Cedar Lumber Association [www.wrcla.org], is for the best example of the exceptional and inventive use of western red cedar from among the awarded projects. Abbe Science Center received the award for the creative cedar siding profile design and its application on a non-residential building.

The architecture makes a modern interpretation of the rural schoolhouse and barn. The exterior western red cedar siding of the one-story classrooms has a stylized corn crib appearance with panelized 1x4 cedar at the entrances, and with nominal 2x4 cedar custom milled in a drop siding pattern that results in a horizontal 1in. channel between siding courses. The protruding upper edges slope 1/8-in. to shed moisture. The siding profile shifts in scale and texture at the two-story lounge with use of horizontal battens at the joints of 1in. thick cedar siding milled with a lower rabbeted edge. The horizontal battens have a 1/8-in. slope and a drip groove. Both siding types are fixed to vertical 1x2 furring with a 3/4-in. air space behind. A pattern of small, rectangular boxed-in windows have visual appeal while offering vignettes of the outdoor landscape.

Millwork consists of maple veneer on medium density fiberboard [MDF] for cabinets, shelving and cubbies, a mahogany slatted bench at the west entrance, and a built-in maple veneer bench in the student lounge.

Jury – A current expression in style and function of the familiar and random arrangement of farm buildings carefully and intimately scaled. The project's craftsmanship and humanity are exposed by fresh, rhythmic patterns of wood siding and fenestration.

Product Specs

Frame
– Slab-on-grade floor, steel frame, standing seam aluminum roof on steel roof deck

Exterior
– Western red cedar siding, custom milled profiles by K+L Millwork, stained marine grade plywood at west entrance, Olympic exterior wood stain

Windows/doors
– Anodized aluminum storefront framing, sliding aluminum and glass doors

Interior
– Western red cedar, tongue and groove in lounge; custom cabinets / shelving / cubbies / exterior bench, maple veneer on medium density fiberboard [MDF] substrate, custom mahogany slatted bench at west entrance, custom maple veneer lounge bench by American Millwork

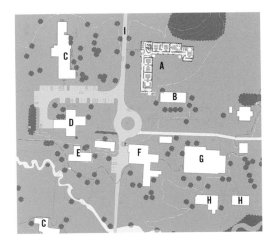

A   Abbe Science Center
B   Library
C   Dorm
D   Cafeteria
E   Office
F   Theater
G   Gymnasium
H   Classroom
I   Entry road

Site plan   0   50   100ft.

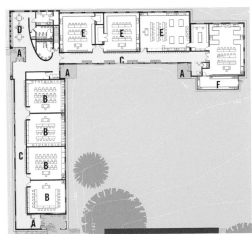

A   Entry
B   General classroom
C   Corridor
D   Student lounge
E   Science classroom
F   Greenhouse

Floor plan   0   12   25ft.

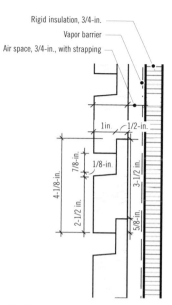

Rigid insulation, 3/4-in.
Vapor barrier
Air space, 3/4-in., with strapping

1in.   1/2-in.

4-1/8-in.

7/8-in.

1/8-in.

3-1/2 in.

2-1/2 in.

5/8-in.

Detail, wood siding one-story construction

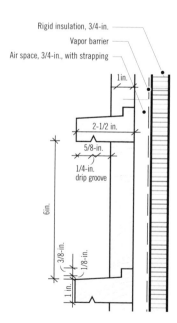

Rigid insulation, 3/4-in.
Vapor barrier
Air space, 3/4-in., with strapping

1in.

2-1/2 in.

5/8-in.

1/4-in.
drip groove

6in.

3/8-in.

1/8-in.

1 in.

Detail, wood siding two-story construction

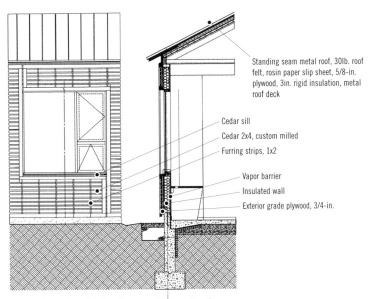

Standing seam metal roof, 30lb. roof felt, rosin paper slip sheet, 5/8-in. plywood, 3in. rigid insulation, metal roof deck

Cedar sill

Cedar 2x4, custom milled

Furring strips, 1x2

Vapor barrier

Insulated wall

Exterior grade plywood, 3/4-in.

Wall section and partial elevation, one-story construction

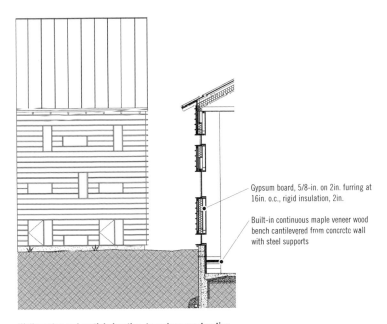

Gypsum board, 5/8-in. on 2in. furring at 16in. o.c., rigid insulation, 2in.

Built-in continuous maple veneer wood bench cantilevered from concrete wall with steel supports

Wall section and partial elevation, two-story construction

Merit Awards

Modular 1 House

STUDIO 804, INC./ DAN ROCKHILL & ASSOCIATES

As part of Studio 804, graduate students in the School of Architecture and Urban Design at the University of Kansas, designed and constructed the Modular 1 House. Studio 804 provides students an avenue to hone design skills and construction knowledge. Modular 1 House responds to the Studio 804 goal of affordable housing solutions through prefabricated construction and modular design. The house represents a viable prototype for modular housing that meets the needs of low and moderate-income households. Wood framing meets the construction and cost efficiencies demanded of prefabrication, and makes a lightweight, durable, structural system for convenient transport.

Each of the five modular units comprising the building is a structural cube of 2x6 exterior walls insulated to R-19, 2x4 partitions and oriented strand board [OSB] sheathing that also provides shear resistance during transport. I-joists in the floor and roof assemblies give a 20-foot clear span that allows for a simplified structure, an open plan, and R-30 insulation. The built-up roof consists of wood strapping, a layer of OSB, and an EPDM roof membrane. The individual modules, built within an enclosed warehouse, were connected on site by bolting through the joist and wall assemblies. Exterior sheathing was infilled between units, followed by EPDM, pressure-treated strapping and a final screen

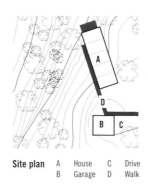

Site plan A House C Drive
B Garage D Walk

horizontal of 1x2 Massaranduba, a Brazilian redwood also known as Bulletwood, that adds an air of richness. Price-competitive and ecologically harvested, Massaranduba is both durable and beautiful. A clear wood finish with an ultra-violet light inhibitor was applied to preserve the natural red color.

The interior of the house modestly continues the wood theme with the inclusion of wood windows, wood cabinetry, and bamboo flooring throughout. The Modular 1 House merges architectural aesthetics, affordable materials, and innovative construction to realize cost and energy efficiencies while redefining the image of the prefabricated house.

Jury – The project demonstrates the clever use of factory-built, mass production technology to lower costs while creating living space of exceptional value. Students learned the process of integrating factory manufacturing with on-site construction, and the selection of materials for aesthetics, durability, renewability, and economy.

Product Specs

Frame
– Lumber framing, 2x6 for walls and 2x4 for partitions, with Simpson Strong Tie gusset plates and hurricane clips used at structural connections, oriented strand board [OSB] glued and nailed to studs for improved shear resistance, TrusJoist TJI-230 I-joists, 20ft. span, for floor and roof sheathed with OSB tongue and groove

Exterior
– Massaranduba 1x2 slats fastened with stainless steel screws to vertical 2x4 strapping, CCA treated, over EPDM membrane, slats finished with Messmoro UV Plus wood finish; roof built-up with wood strapping, a layer of OSB, and an EPDM roof membrane with 1/4-in. drainage slope; Massaranduba 1x6 at entrance ramp and rear deck

Interior
– Gypsum board with aluminum paneling, bamboo flooring, eucalyptus cabinetry with bamboo trim

Windows/doors
– Clad wood windows and sliding doors, translucent polycarbonate panels for end cap fenestration; wood frame constructed doors with aluminum paneling

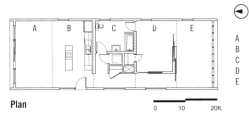

A   Living unit
B   Kitchen unit
C   Bath/utility unit
D   Bedroom unit
E   Study unit

Plan

0   10   20ft.

Section looking west

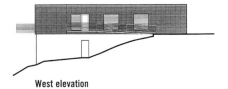

West elevation

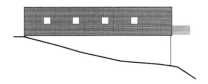

South elevation

Wood framing is fast, light in weight, and economical, and tolerances are easy to maintain, all essential qualities for prefabrication. The modules are structurally independent, then combined on site into a continuous structural unit.

End walls removed after transport to site.

Module ready for connection.

Modules bolted together and seams filled with OSB sheathing and the rainscreen wall.

Temporary 2x4 end walls with OSB sheathing close off the modules and provide racking resistance during transport. On site, the end walls are removed and used to build the garage. Bolt connections join the modules and the gaps filled with the rain screen wall system.

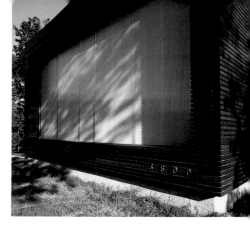

Roof:

Membrane, EPDM
OSB, 1/2-in.
Wood blocking
I-joist, 2-5/16 x 11-7/8
Insulation, batt
Gypsum board, 1/2-in.

Bolt, 1/2-in.
Wood blocking
OSB, two layers @ 1/2-in.
Double top plate

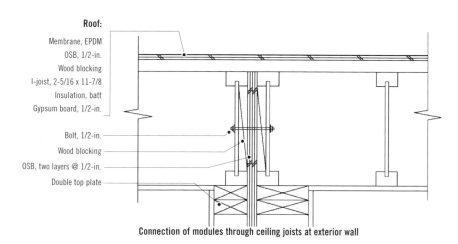

Connection of modules through ceiling joists at exterior wall

Floor:

Bamboo flooring, T&G
Plywood, 3/4-in.
I-joist, 2-5/16 x 11-7/8
Insulation, batt

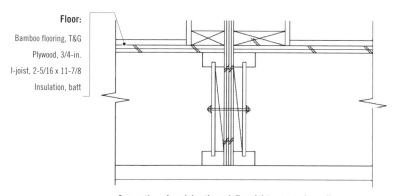

Connection of modules through floor joists at exterior wall

CLIENT
City Vision Ministries
Kansas City, Kansas

ARCHITECTS
Studio 804, Project Team
Dan Rockhill, design and construction
Kent Spreckelmeyer, project management

CONSULTANTS
Scott Murray, Unified Government of
Wyandotte County
Jonathan Birkel, City Vision Ministries

STRUCTURAL ENGINEER
Norton & Schmidt Consulting Engineers
Kansas City, Kansas

GENERAL CONTRACTOR
Studio 804, Inc./ Dan Rockhill
Lawrence, Kansas

PHOTOS
Dan Rockhill
Lawrence, Kansas

Yin Yu Tang House

JOHN G. WAITE ASSOCIATES, ARCHITECTS

Yin Yu Tang [Hall of Plentiful Shelter] is a 200-year-old, 4,500sf merchant's house from southeastern China that was disassembled, shipped to the United States, and re-erected at the Peabody Essex Museum in Salem, Massachusetts. The project set new standards for historic preservation scholarship and practice, resulting in opportunities for people in North America to learn about Chinese architecture, art and history.

The architectural goal of the project was to retain the historic fabric of the building while preserving its centuries-old character. The house has the traditional style of the Huizhou region of China: timber frame supporting an unglazed tile roof with a sandstone foundation, brick walls, and a white lime exterior. Beyond the structural frame, wood forms the floors, ceilings, partition walls, doors, window sash and frames, and elaborately carved interior screens.

New woodwork was required to be visually consistent with the historic character of the house. Repair work using traditional techniques was marked discreetly to distinguish it from the historic building fabric and can be reversed to allow for new restoration technologies in the future. The timber frame was re-erected using traditional joinery methods, and new components used only where elements were missing or severely damaged.

Construction modifications to meet code life-safety and seismic requirements have minimal effect on the historic fabric of the house. A new basement under the building houses mechanical and electrical equipment necessary for use as a year-round museum. A new elevator and stair tower annex maintains the wood theme with bamboo flooring in the lobbies and cork flooring and cypress paneling in the elevator cab.

Within the house, wood partitions were blind-hinged to provide an accessible path through the first floor. The roof was carefully retrofitted with a marine plywood diaphragm to resist seismic loading and to provide a base for membrane roofing that was sandwiched between the original layers of Chinese roof tile. A seasonal skylight protects the courtyard during winter and is removed in the spring.

Jury – An astonishing reassembly of a venerable, historic building where new and old wood components combine to make an educational and cultural tour de force. The building craft of the past demonstrates to a new generation that noble wood structures be saved and re-used.

Product Specs

Frame
– Original 18th Century timber frame with traditional repairs and component replacement, original structural plank flooring with traditional repairs, original rafter framing supporting tile roofing; original non-structural wood panel and brick partitions

CLIENT
Peabody-Essex Museum, Salem,
Massachusetts/ Brookfield Arts
Foundation, Boston, Massachusetts

ARCHITECT
John G. Waite Associates, Architects
Albany, New York

STRUCTURAL ENGINEER
ARUP
Cambridge, Massachusetts

GENERAL CONTRACTOR
Liberty Street Restoration Company
Albany, New York

PHOTO
John G. Waite Associates, Architects
Albany, New York/
Richard Howard, Photographer

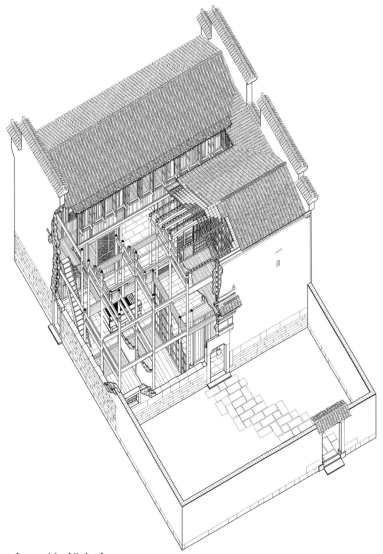

**Axonometric of timber frame
and masonry wall construction.**
[Drawing by John G. Waite Associates, Architects]

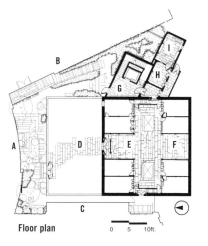

A   Museum atrium
B   Museum auditorium
C   Museum gallery
D   Forecourt
E   Lower Hall
F   Upper Hall
G   Elevator and fire stair
H   Kitchen
I   Gong tower

Floor plan

0   5   10ft.

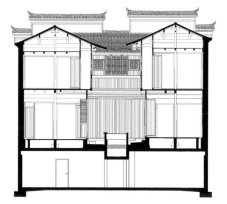

Transverse building section looking east, including
mechanical space in new basement.

Above: The timber frame has 62 round columns joined by rectangular beams using traditional mortise-and-tenon joinery techniques.

Many beams were fabricated from smaller pieces held together with free tenons, a technique that demonstrated the craftsman's skills, and because of the time required, the importance of the building's owner.

Below: The entire rear half of a beam could be deteriorated from contact with masonry. Deteriorated areas were removed with an adze and the remaining sound areas splined to a new beam of yellow pine.

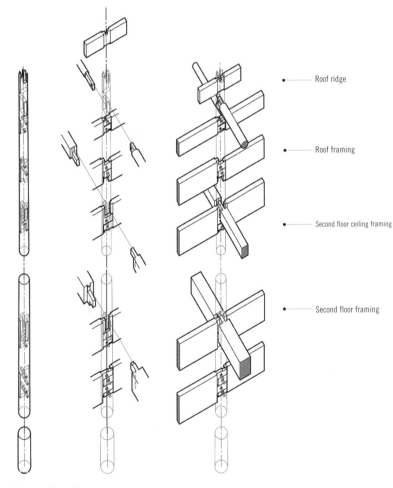

- Roof ridge

- Roof framing

- Second floor ceiling framing

- Second floor framing

Column and beam joinery

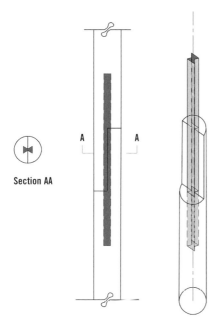

Section AA

Column scarf joint assembly.

A 90-cm long bladed and nosed scarf, with a wooden dovetail key inserted the full length of the scarf, joins old and new without need for external pins or bolts. The metal pipe clamps [below] were used during transport and then removed.

Bottom: Early growth American woods, such as pine and cypress, that were similar in character and strength to the original Chinese wood, were used for beam and column repairs.

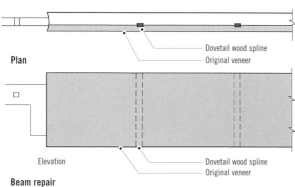

Plan

— Dovetail wood spline
— Original veneer

☐

Elevation — Dovetail wood spline
— Original veneer

Beam repair

Citation Awards

Sauna Pavilion

WEBSTER WILSON ARCHITECT

Inspired by his study of wood construction in Finland on a Valle Scholarship, graduate student Webster Wilson designed and built a sauna as his master's thesis in architecture at the University of Washington. In its details and use of wood, the project demonstrates a durable and compelling model of wood construction for the timber-rich region of the northwest.

Every detail and piece of wood was carefully thought through to assure breathability and water drainage. Clear western red cedar was used for siding and decking, select structural Douglas fir for framing, and stainless steel for hardware and fasteners. Lexan plastic, 10mm thick and screwed to 2x3 furring on the double fir rafters, serves as the roof. The walls, floor and roof enclosing the steaming room are designed as breathable cavities with no sheathing. Water vapor readily passes through the wood fiber insulation imported from Finland

The 10ft. x 24ft. footprint of the building includes the steaming room and a covered deck and changing area. The building was designed without a specific site in mind, but was intended to sit lightly in a wooded landscape on six concrete piers. The design concept involved inserting a finely crafted wooden box into an exposed timber frame. Much of the final aesthetic evolved from the need for the building to be a kit of parts in which wall panels insert into the framing assembly by screwing through a 2x2 scab on the wall to a similar scab on the studs.

The sauna was exhibited at the university for three months before being re-erected near Langely, Whidbey Island for a private client who helped select a site among 70-year old second growth fir trees. With many years of service ahead of it, the sauna will gracefully recede into the forest from which it came.

Jury – A modest building delicately sited in the trees, the student project shows great care in the means and methods of wood construction. Every board, its size and location, has been considered.

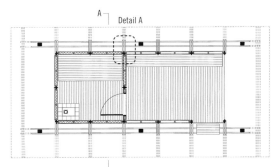

Floor plan

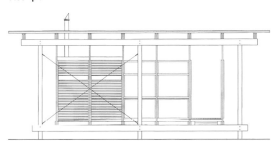

Front elevation

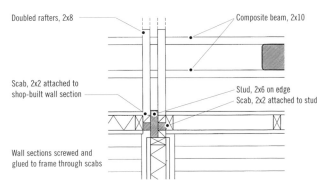

Doubled rafters, 2x8

Composite beam, 2x10

Scab, 2x2 attached to
shop-built wall section

Stud, 2x6 on edge
Scab, 2x2 attached to stud

Wall sections screwed and
glued to frame through scabs

Detail A, wall to wall connection

Product Specs

Frame
– Double Douglas fir rafters, 2x8 and
double floor joists, 2x6 on 4ft. centers,
supported on composite beams of
double 2x10 and glulam columns,
stainless steel marine hardware and
cable bracing; roof of Lexan plastic,
10mm thick, fastened to 2x3 furring on
double rafters with neoprene washer
and hexagonal screws

Exterior
– Western red cedar siding, nominal 1x3
milled with angled top and bottom
edges, finished with Daly's "Sea Fin"
marine teak oil

Windows
Custom Douglas fir windows and door
with tempered insulated glass

Interior
Western red cedar ceiling and benches,
slate floor, stainless steel panels near
stove

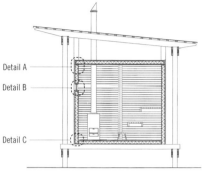

Section A-A

Detail A
Detail B
Detail C

ARCHITECT
Webster Wilson
Seattle, Washington

GENERAL CONTRACTOR
Webster Wilson
Seattle, Washington

PHOTOS
John Granen
Seattle, WA
[all photos except as noted below]
Mark Wilson
West Cornwall, Connecticut
[p. 66, 72 top]

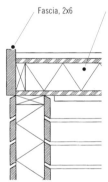

Fascia, 2x6

Ceiling: cedar 1x4 top and bottom, plywood 1/2-in. top and bottom, ceiling joists 2x4 @ 16in. o.c., wood fiber insulation, black 30lb. roofing felt both sides of insulation

Detail A, section wall to wall

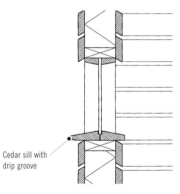

Cedar sill with drip groove

Detail B, window

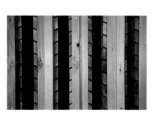

Pre-built wall sections
Note the 2x2 scabs on the ends that facilitate attachment of the wall sections to similar scabs on the 2x6 studs.

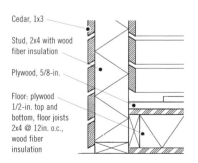

Cedar, 1x3

Stud, 2x4 with wood fiber insulation

Plywood, 5/8-in.

Floor: plywood 1/2-in. top and bottom, floor joists 2x4 @ 12in. o.c., wood fiber insulation

Detail C, wall to floor

Jackson Meadow

SALMELA ARCHITECT AND COEN + STUMPF + ASSOCIATES

Marine on St. Croix, population 602, the oldest town in Minnesota, was founded on the logging industry. Jackson Meadow, a development of cedar-clad, wood frame houses stained white, is built on the last development land in the town.

With the consent of the local planning authorities, the project reserves two thirds of the land for green space, and the remainder for 64 individual, custom designed homes. There are numerous environmental innovations, such as two wetland septic systems and a centralized pump house for well water in place of individual systems, but the most visually significant aspect is the architectural strength of the complex.

Two simple, historic houses in the original town became the mean from which five rules were established to maintain a consistent scale, form, material and color :

1. All buildings to be wood frame and wood clad,
2. All buildings to be less than 24ft. in width,
3. All garages to be detached with up to four outbuildings allowed per lot,
4. All roofs to be 12/12 pitch in standing metal seam galvalume, and
5. All buildings to be white, except utility buildings to be black.

The result is a modernist abstraction of the traditional village one might encounter in the mid-West and New England. The assembly of white wood

buildings has a poetic quality that relates contextually to the historic Marine on St. Croix, but is never saccharine. It is through the simplification of highly familiar details – neutral white stain on 1x4 and 1x6 beveled, and board and batten siding, and 2x trim boards milled with sharp edges – that the architecture connects the traditional and the modern. Maple floors and cabinetry are standard for the interiors.

The principle of using common materials in a common vernacular building form applied to all types of building requirements, is the same concept that makes the memorable hill towns of Europe, the hamlets of the British Isles, and the unique villages of Scandinavia so dear to the world.

Jury – Drawn from the Scandinavian roots of northern Minnesota, the housing development is assembled as a village with conversation between houses, and serves as a model for other developers. Houses are set directly on the prairie, rather than merging with it, so that the two co-habit in a delicate balance. Details such as asymmetric gable roofs, and cut-outs in facades, are playful and inventive.

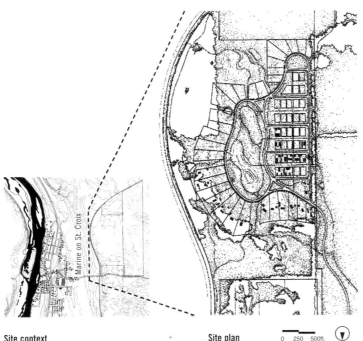

Site context   Site plan   0 250 500ft.

Marine on St. Croix

Product Specs

Frame
– Platform frame wood construction, conventional and scissor wood roof trusses

Exterior
– Western red cedar siding, 1x4 and 1x6 beveled, board and batten siding, batten on plywood siding, 2x trim boards milled with sharp edges for strong shadow lines, all stained white except utility buildings stained black; standing seam galvalume roofing

Windows
– Metal-clad wood windows and exterior doors by Loewen

Interior
– Maple floors and cabinetry, trim, paneling, interior wood doors
Cost/sf: varies $150 to $250

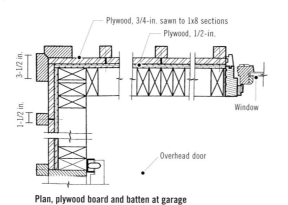

Plywood, 3/4-in. sawn to 1x8 sections

Plywood, 1/2-in.

3-1/2 in.

1-1/2 in.

Window

Overhead door

Plan, plywood board and batten at garage

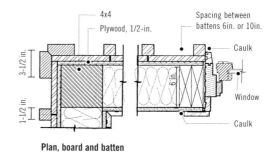

4x4

Plywood, 1/2-in.

Spacing between battens 6in. or 10in.

Caulk

3-1/2 in.

1-1/2 in.

6 in.

Window

Caulk

Plan, board and batten

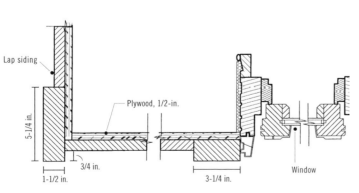

Lap siding

Plywood, 1/2-in.

5-1/4 in.

3/4 in.

1-1/2 in.

3-1/4 in.

Window

Plan, lap siding at sauna

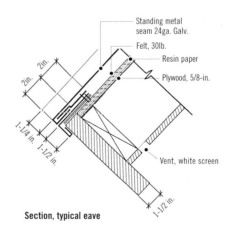

Standing metal
seam 24ga. Galv.

Felt, 30lb.

Resin paper

Plywood, 5/8-in.

2in.

2in.

1-1/4 in.

1-1/2 in.

Vent, white screen

1-1/2 in.

Section, typical eave

CLIENT
Harold Teasdale/ Robert Durphey
Minneapolis, Minnesota

ARCHITECT
Salmela Architect
Duluth, Minnesota

STRUCTURAL ENGINEER
Carroll Franck & Associates
St. Paul, Minnesota

GENERAL CONTRACTOR
Cates Construction
Stillwater, Minnesota

LANDSCAPE ARCHITECT
Coen + Stumpf + Associates
Minneapolis, MN

PHOTOS
Peter Bastianelli-Kerze
Eveleth, Minnesota

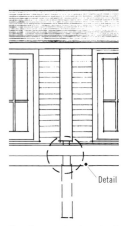

Detail

Elevation, porch column to pier

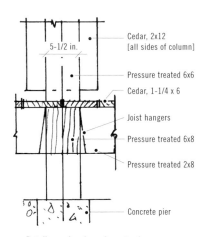

5-1/2 in.

Cedar, 2x12 [all sides of column]

Pressure treated 6x6

Cedar, 1-1/4 x 6

Joist hangers

Pressure treated 6x8

Pressure treated 2x8

Concrete pier

Detail, porch column base to pier

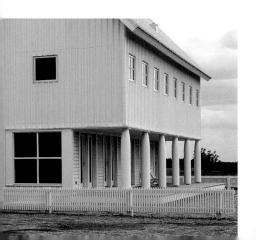

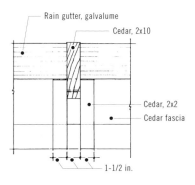

Rain gutter, galvalume

Cedar, 2x10

Cedar, 2x2

Cedar fascia

1-1/2 in.

Plan, gutter support

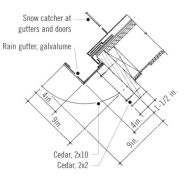

Snow catcher at gutters and doors

Rain gutter, galvalume

4 in.

9 in.

1-1/2 in.

4 in.

9 in.

Cedar, 2x10

Cedar, 2x2

Section, gutter support

The Kate and Laurance Eustis Chapel

ESKEW + DUMEZ + RIPPLE

The 1,000sf inter-denominational chapel, commissioned by the Ochsner Clinic Foundation in New Orleans, replaces an existing hospital chapel that lacked both ceremonial presence and religious character. The new chapel is a place for personal meditation, and provides the traditional peace and sanctuary of religious architecture.

The darkened entry vestibule begins the ritualistic sequence of spaces that typically anticipate places of prayer. The chapel consists of a main worship space with seating for 12, and two private meditation rooms.

Upon entering, the devices of light, scale, proportion and material treatments transport one out of the institutional hospital environment and into a realm of the senses. The use of wood, particularly the "shroud" that hovers over visitors as a luminescent curtain, brings tactile warmth. Daylight from a concealed window illuminates a channel of fountain water that drops into a basin beneath an altar of cast glass tablets. The sound of water has a calming effect that alludes to its healing, life-giving properties.

The shroud consists of Spanish Cedar finished with catalyzed lacquer, and built of 1x2 runners of various lengths, and 1/4-in. x 1x12 slats. The slats are glued into dadoes cut on 11° angles into the runners. The result is alternating rows of slats and runners assembled in 1ft. wide panel sections. Rods, extending from a grid of metal uni-strut, thread into wooden strongbacks. Screws pass through slots cut in the strongbacks and into the runners of the shroud. The screws can move laterally to accommodate any movement of the shroud. Where the wall and ceiling shrouds meet the runners inter-weave in the manner of interlocking fingers. The wall component of the shroud is also screwed to strongbacks and stands about 6in. off the wall. The metal brackets of the glass altar fasten back through the runners to the concrete wall with the slats installed after. Hardwood used consists of ebony-stained oak flooring, cherry benches, and cherry panels in the meditation rooms.

Jury – An imaginative detailing of wood seemingly woven as a textile that transforms the hospital environment into a quiet retreat. Light penetrating the wooden shroud has an ethereal effect, providing an intimately enclosed space that does not confine the meditator.

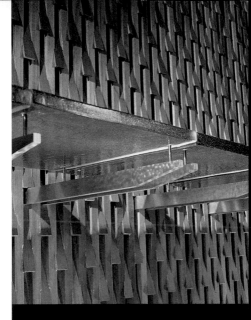

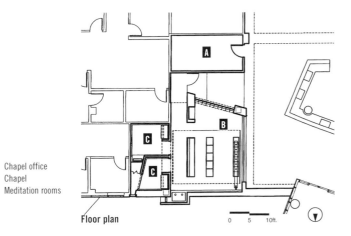

A   Chapel office
B   Chapel
C   Meditation rooms

Floor plan   0   5   10ft.

Steel rod, threaded

Steel bracket

Wood strongback

Horizontal wood frame,
1x2

Wood slats 1/4-in. thick

Gypsum wall board

Vertical wood frame,
1x2

Steel tube 3/4 x 1-1/2
between steel bars and
anchored to wall

Steel bar, 1/2 x 1-1/2

Glass altar with 1/4-in.
steel support rods

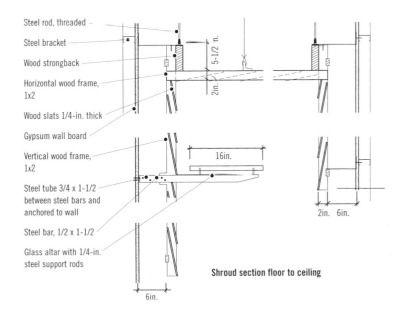

Shroud section floor to ceiling

Product Specs

Interior
– Shroud of Spanish Cedar finished with
catalyzed lacquer, built of 1x2 runners of
various lengths, and 1/4-in. x 1x12 slats,
slats glued into dadoes cut on 11°
angles into the runners, slats and
runners assembled into 1ft. wide panel
sections; entry wall of Spanish Cedar and
glass; furnishings cherry, cherry veneer
plywood as wainscoting in meditation
rooms; oak floors stained ebony

Project Area
– 1,000sf

Construction Cost
– $230,000

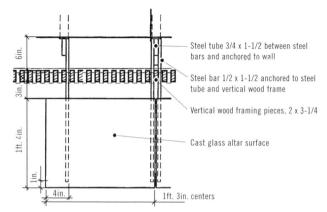

Steel tube 3/4 x 1-1/2 between steel bars and anchored to wall

Steel bar 1/2 x 1-1/2 anchored to steel tube and vertical wood frame

Vertical wood framing pieces, 2 x 3-1/4

Cast glass altar surface

6in.

3in.

1ft. 4in.

1in.

4in.

1ft. 3in. centers

Plan at glass altar

CLIENT
Ochsner Clinic Foundation
New Orleans, Louisiana

ARCHITECT
Eskew+Dumez+Ripple
New Orleans, Louisiana

GENERAL CONTRACTOR
Construction South
New Orleans, Louisiana

MILLWORK
Axis Construction,
New Orleans, Louisiana

PHOTOS
Timothy Hursley
Little Rock, Arkansas
[p. 82, 83, 86, 88 top]
Neil Alexander
New Orleans, Louisiana
[p. 84, 85, 87, 88 bottom, 89]

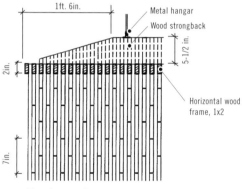

1ft. 6in.

Metal hangar

Wood strongback

5-1/2 in.

2in.

Horizontal wood frame, 1x2

7in.

Elevation at ceiling

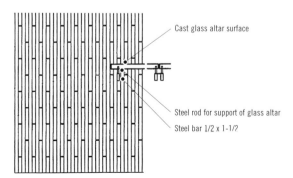

Cast glass altar surface

Steel rod for support of glass altar

Steel bar 1/2 x 1-1/2

Elevation at glass altar

Canopy Colonnade
ARTHUR ERICKSON ARCHITECTURAL CORP./ NICK MILKOVICH ARCHITECTS INC.

The concept of this project lies in a response to minimize and consolidate the scale between the pedestrian and the massive size of the 'big box' retail structures. In addition to locating the retail buildings against the valley slope, the solution was to create a covered colonnade canopy structure that would become the dominant relief element, and that would unify and connect the expression of the two retailers.

The column and branch articulation of the colonnade structural elements responds to the strong influence of the Aspen forests of the surrounding landscape. Lower down the columns, transparent screens accommodate store signs and offer another level of interest at the pedestrian scale. The screens and branch-like structure of the south-facing colonnade create playful shadow patterns on the store fronts. The coffered wood canopy structure contrasts and adds warmth to the concrete store fronts and is amplified at night through accent lighting located at the junctions of the struts.

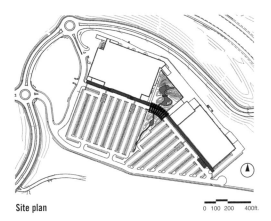

Site plan

0 100 200   400ft.

The tree-like supports consist of 21ft. high, 14in. diameter columns spaced at 20ft. and 10ft. centers. Angled steel struts, 3-1/2 in. in diameter, extend 10ft. terminating at a horizontal steel plate that bolts to the underside of the timber canopy assembly. The canopy construction is a 5ft.-square grid of doubled 3-1/8 x12 glued-laminated beams and purlins that connect with through bolts, steel plates and glulam rivets. The roof is built-up 2x6 tongue and groove Douglas fir decking, rigid insulation tapered to link the drainage to the roof drainage systems of the stores, and roof membrane.

Taking advantage of existing natural features of the site, a park-like setting was created between the stores extending through the parking lots on the south slope and emphasizing the connection of the site to a nearby green belt.

Jury – Wood makes a welcoming transition for people moving from the parking lot to the impersonal big box store, thus making the project a civic place in "nowheresville". The wood canopy reflects light and projects warmth, an effect enhanced at night with up-lighting.

Product Specs

Frame

– Canopy supports 21ft. high, 14in. diameter columns spaced at 20ft. and 10ft. centers, angled steel struts, 3-1/2 in. in dia. extend 10ft. and bolt to the underside of doubled 3-1/8 x12 glued-laminated beams and purlins set on a 5ft.-square grid, beam to purlin connections consist of thru bolts, A307 3/4-in. diameter with 3/8-in. bolts, steel plates and Simpson Strong Drive screws, 1/4-in. dia. x 3in. long; roof built-up 2x6, tongue and groove Douglas fir decking, tapered rigid insulation and membrane

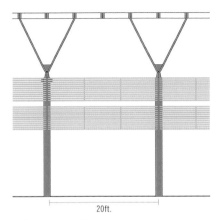

20ft.

Typical front elevation

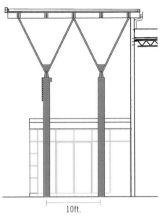

10ft.

Typical side elevation at store entry

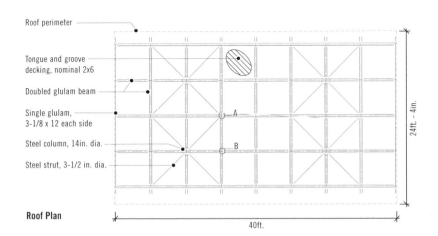

Roof perimeter

Tongue and groove
decking, nominal 2x6

Doubled glulam beam

Single glulam,
3-1/8 x 12 each side

Steel column, 14in. dia.

Steel strut, 3-1/2 in. dia.

A

B

24ft. - 4in.

Roof Plan

40ft.

CLIENT
Traer Creek, LLC
Avon, Colorado

ARCHITECT
Arthur Erickson Architectural Corporation/
Nick Milkovich Architects Inc.
Vancouver, British Columbia

ARCHITECT AND STRUCTURAL ENGINEER
CASCO [Engineer Home Depot], St. Louis,
Missouri; BSW Architects [Engineer
Wal-Mart], Tulsa, Oklahoma

DESIGN ENGINEER
Fast + Epp Structural Engineers
Vancouver, British Columbia

PHOTOS
Cameron Owen, Design Workshop
Aspen, Colorado

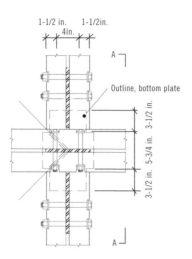

1-1/2 in. 1-1/2in.
4in.

A

Outline, bottom plate

3-1/2 in.
3-1/2 in.
5-3/4 in.
3-1/2 in.

A

Node A from roof plan: Plan, purlin to beam connection at struts

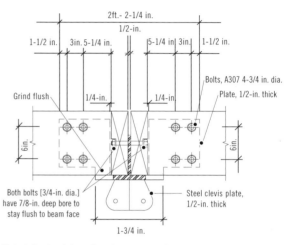

2ft.- 2-1/4 in.
1/2-in.

1-1/2 in. 3in. 5-1/4 in.   5-1/4 in. 3in. 1-1/2 in.

Grind flush   1/4-in.   1/4-in.   Bolts, A307 4-3/4 in. dia.
Plate, 1/2-in. thick

6in.   6in.

Both bolts [3/4-in. dia.] have 7/8-in. deep bore to stay flush to beam face

Steel clevis plate, 1/2-in. thick

1-3/4 in.

Node A: Section A-A, purlin to beam connection at struts

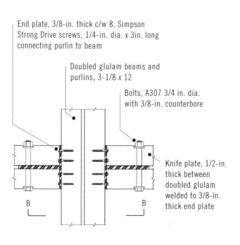

End plate, 3/8-in. thick c/w 8, Simpson Strong Drive screws, 1/4-in. dia. x 3in. long connecting purlin to beam

Doubled glulam beams and purlins, 3-1/8 x 12

Bolts, A307 3/4 in. dia. with 3/8-in. counterbore

Knife plate, 1/2-in. thick between doubled glulam welded to 3/8-in. thick end plate

B   B

Node B from roof plan: Plan, purlin to beam connection

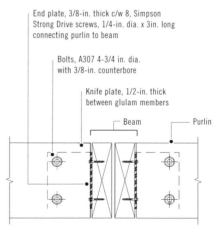

End plate, 3/8-in. thick c/w 8, Simpson Strong Drive screws, 1/4-in. dia. x 3in. long connecting purlin to beam

Bolts, A307 4-3/4 in. dia. with 3/8-in. counterbore

Knife plate, 1/2-in. thick between glulam members

Beam   Purlin

Node B: Section B-B, purlin to beam connection

Garden Pavilion

PAUL RAFF STUDIO

Sitting in the backyard of a residential lot, the pavilion serves a range of activities from a private place to public meetings and performances of the local Artists' Garden Cooperative, a group that connects its activities to the urban garden atmosphere. The client wanted the pavilion to have a strong architectural theme as a focal point for the garden and as a backdrop for performances, but at the same time to connect sky to earth in a delicate interplay of light and shadow.

The form responds to the narrow garden site and to the strategy of shading the rays of the mid-afternoon sun while also maximizing views to the sky, thus the structure angles toward the highest point of the sun. There is an intentional kinship with traditional Japanese forms, such as the gently bowing roof, that evoke grace and calm.

The pavilion is a low maintenance structure built of economical and naturally durable knotty grade 2x4 cedar used in a type of rhythmic lattice construction that elevates the 2x4 to an aesthetic abstraction. It touches the land lightly, with a compact, partly cantilevered footprint resting on four foundation columns.

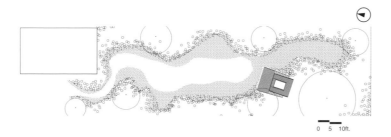

Framing pieces are set 4in. o.c. The double framing layers of the wall and glazed roof create an ambiguous sense of depth. In the walls, one structural layer tilts outward to make a comfortable back support for built-in seating, and the outer layer of framing tilts south in the same direction as the uplifted roof. The two framing layers bring rigidity and eliminate the need for cross-bracing. The upper layer of the trellis roof acts in compression and the curved 1x4 lower members, held in alignment by a steel tension cable that crosses at mid-span, are in tension. The framing method creates a taut structure, both physically and visually. Computer generated measurements were used to guide the precise cutting of lengths and angles required.

Jury – The project achieves maximum effect with minimal means through the use of economy-grade knotty cedar carefully placed and connected to serve both structurally and ornamentally. The structure is appropriately delicate as a place for outdoor social gatherings.

Product Specs

Frame
– Knotty cedar 2x4 and 1x4; Lexan roof with custom stainless steel clips

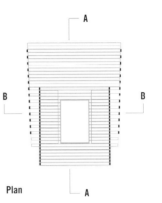

Plan

Section B-B

Front elevation

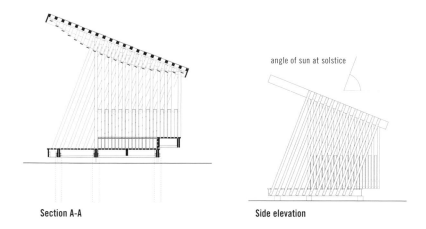

Section A-A

angle of sun at solstice

Side elevation

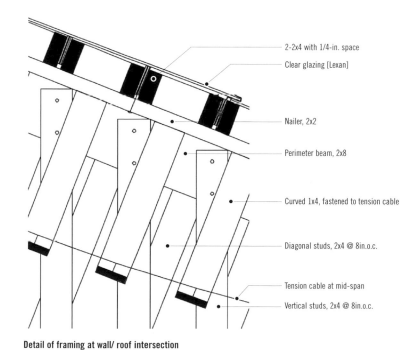

2-2x4 with 1/4-in. space

Clear glazing [Lexan]

Nailer, 2x2

Perimeter beam, 2x8

Curved 1x4, fastened to tension cable

Diagonal studs, 2x4 @ 8in.o.c.

Tension cable at mid-span

Vertical studs, 2x4 @ 8in.o.c.

Detail of framing at wall/ roof intersection

CLIENT
Susan Brown
Toronto, Ontario

ARCHITECT
Paul Raff Studio Inc.
Toronto, Ontario

DESIGN ENGINEER
Sasquatch
Toronto, Ontario

GENERAL CONTRACTOR
Sasquatch
Toronto, Ontario

Minton Hill House

AFFLECK + DE LA RIVA ARCHITECTS

The 1,700sf house for a single resident situated on a hilltop in Quebec's picturesque Eastern Townships strikes a balance between being open to the grand views and providing a protective domestic environment.

There are four main components: the roof, the stone hearth, the wood shell and the sun window. Supported on a series of slender steel column and beam frames surmounted by two layers of parallel-chord trusses, the roof celebrates the hill top position of the house with a spread-wing profile that separates land and sky. With a narrow soffit on the north and a generous overhang on the south, the roof gives solar control characteristic of traditional area farmhouses, but in a contemporary architectural form.

The stone hearth is a 90° folded plate of slate that cradles the living and dining areas and provides some environmental control with its southerly orientation. In summer, the roof overhang protects against the sun and the stone hearth provides cooling to the living area. When the sun is low in winter, the hearth becomes a solar collector aided by a hot water coil under the floor's concrete slab

The 2x4 wood frame cedar-clad shell at both ends of the house, and at the open end of the stone hearth, contains the more private areas – bedrooms, bathrooms, and home office – the "psychologically defensible" spaces on an exposed and vulnerable site. The sun window opens the southern wall of the house to the landscape.

The wood shell and exterior of the stone hearth combine on the north side, the main approach to the house, to form a horizontal screen that gradually reveals the panoramic view while shielding the house from northern weather. The home office is pulled away from the main body of the house, a traditional Japanese device, creating an exterior passage that makes indoor-outdoor movement part of the living experience of the house. Interior finishes include cherry plywood millwork and birch floors.

Jury – A simple, beautifully proportioned house in which wood does not overpower. The contrast with green stone and glass makes the wood feel warmer. Floating on slender steel columns above the open interior, the planar wood ceiling warms the space below with simple grace.

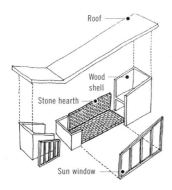

Schematic of components

Roof

Wood shell

Stone hearth

Sun window

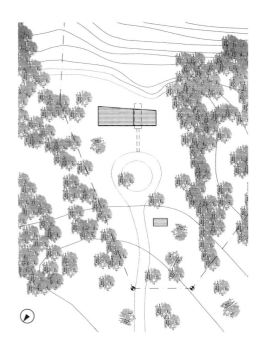

Site Plan

Product Specs

Frame

– Concrete crawl space, min. 5ft., steel frames on 15ft. to 17ft. centers supporting double layer of parallel chord roof trusses 24in. o.c.: lower 3-1/2 x 20 with 10in. batt insulation, upper 3-1/2 x 14-1/2 open for ventilation, tongue and groove 3/4-in. plywood sheathing, 5/8-in. fiberboard, elastomeric membrane; 2x4 insulated wall construction, plywood sheathing, extruded polystyrene, wood furring strips, pre-finished bevel cedar siding

Interior

– Pine ceilings, birch floors second level, slate first level, birch stair treads, cherry cabinetry

Windows/Doors

– Spanish cedar doors by Prodomo, Lachine, QC, aluminum doors

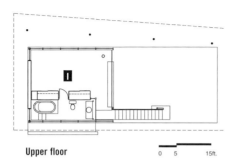

Upper floor

0 5   15ft.

A   Exterior passage
B   Entry
C   Kitchen
D   Dining and living
E   Guest bedroom
F   Utility room
G   Home office
H   Screened porch
I   Master bedroom
J   Lookout

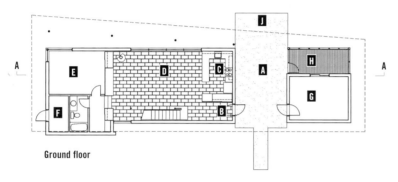

Ground floor

South elevation

Section A-A

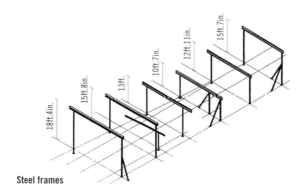

Steel frames

18ft.4in.
15ft.8in.
13ft.
10ft.7in.
12ft.11in.
15ft.7in.

CLIENT
Steve Marien
North Hatley, Quebec

ARCHITECT
Affleck + de la Riva Architects
Montreal, Quebec

STRUCTURAL ENGINEER
Comtois, Blouin and Associates Consulting
Structural Engineers
Montreal, Quebec

GENERAL CONTRACTOR
RG Construction
North Hatley, Quebec

PHOTOS
Marc Cramer Photographer
Montreal, Quebec

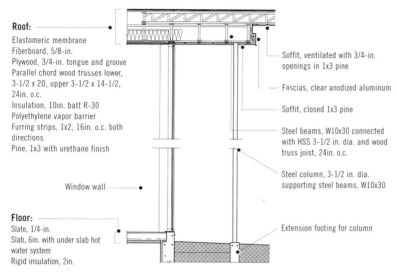

Roof:
Elastomeric membrane
Fiberboard, 5/8-in.
Plywood, 3/4-in. tongue and groove
Parallel chord wood trusses lower,
3-1/2 x 20, upper 3-1/2 x 14-1/2,
24in. o.c.
Insulation, 10in. batt R-30
Polyethylene vapor barrier
Furring strips, 1x2, 16in. o.c. both
directions
Pine, 1x3 with urethane finish

Window wall

Floor:
Slate, 1/4-in.
Slab, 6in. with under slab hot
water system
Rigid insulation, 2in.

Soffit, ventilated with 3/4-in.
openings in 1x3 pine

Fascias, clear anodized aluminum

Soffit, closed 1x3 pine

Steel beams, W10x30 connected
with HSS 3-1/2 in. dia. and wood
truss joist, 24in. o.c.

Steel column, 3-1/2 in. dia.
supporting steel beams, W10x30

Extension footing for column

Section through roof overhang, south wall

Using two layers of parallel chord roof trusses, one on top of the other, provides the depth for adequate insulation and ventilation, while the pronounced overhangs present a thinner roof profile. To form the roof overhangs, short lengths of trusses run 90° to the main roof trusses.

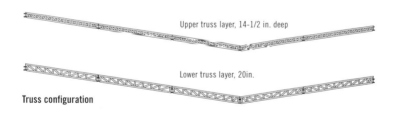

Upper truss layer, 14-1/2 in. deep

Lower truss layer, 20in.

Truss configuration

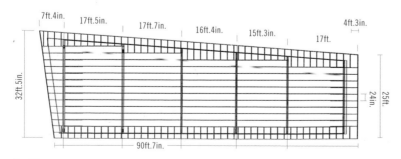

7ft.4in. 17ft.5in. 17ft.7in. 16ft.4in. 15ft.3in. 17ft. 4ft.3in.

32ft.5in. 25ft. 24in.

90ft.7in.

Roof framing

ALSO BY TUNS PRESS

Architecture Canada 2004 : The Governor General's Medals in Architecture
ISBN 0-929112-51-2, 2004

Saucier + Perrotte Architectes, 1995-2002
ISBN 0-929112-46-6, 2004

The Wood Design Awards 2003 : A North American Program of Architectural Excellence
ISBN 0-929112-50-4, 2003

Barry Johns Architects : Selected Projects 1984-1998
ISBN 0-929112-32-6, 2000

Brian MacKay-Lyons : Selected Projects 1986-1997
ISBN 0-929112-39-3, 1998

Works : The Architecture of A.J. Diamond, Donald Schmitt & Company, 1968-1995
ISBN 0-929112-31-8, 1996

Patkau Architects : Selected Projects 1983-1993
ISBN 0-929112-28-8, 1994

For additional information, please see our website at tunspress.dal.ca.

For the Wood Design Awards information and registration: www.WoodDesignAwards.com.